Because I Cannot Leave This Body

Because
I Cannot
Leave
This Body

CAROL V. DAVIS

New Odyssey Series
Truman State University Press
Kirksville, Missouri

Copyright © 2017 Carol V. Davis/Truman State University Press, Kirksville, Missouri 63501
All rights reserved
tsup.truman.edu

Cover art: Yvette M. Brown, *Anna*, oil on canvas, 2006. Used with permission of the artist.
Cover design: Lisa Ahrens

Library of Congress Cataloging-in-Publication Data

Names: Davis, Carol V., author.
Title: Because I cannot leave this body / Carol V. Davis.
Description: Kirksville, MO : Truman State University Press, [2016] | Series: New odyssey series
Identifiers: LCCN 2016048479 (print) | LCCN 2016052041 (ebook) | ISBN 9781612481883 (softcover : acid-free paper) | ISBN 9781612481890
Classification: LCC PS3604.A9558 A6 2017 (print) | LCC PS3604.A9558 (ebook) |
    DDC 811/.6-dc23
LC record available at https://lccn.loc.gov/2016048479

No part of this work may be reproduced or transmitted in any format by any means without written permission from the publisher.

The paper in this publication meets or exceeds the minimum requirements of the American National Standard for Information Sciences—Permanence of Paper for Printed Library Materials, ANSI Z39.48–1992.

for Chuck

Without conversations, memories turn into stones or fairy tales.

—Svetlana Boym

Contents

Acknowledgments | xi

I   The Edge of Things | 2
Sentries | 3
Dare | 4
Coneflower | 5
Flying off the Page | 6
Animal Time | 8
Predicting Weather | 9
Long Shadows | 10
Hollowed Fruit | 11
What Followed | 12
The Equation | 13
Late January, Wyoming Storm | 14

II   Speaking in Tongues | 18
What Really Happened | 20
Contemplating Murder | 21
Betrayal | 23
Money Laundering | 24
Into the Forest | 26
Humor | 27
Because One and the Other | 28

What I'd Ban | 29
The Dog Show | 30
John Bower, Biologist, Explains Bird Calls | 31
Let Rust Take Its Rightful Place | 33
This Is Where We Stand | 34
Because the Porchlight Flickered | 35

III

Because | 38
Black Hat | 40
Even Now | 41
A Watched Pot | 42
Again the Crows | 44
The Day It Changed | 45
On the Eve of Yom Kippur, I Listen to the Rachmaninoff Vespers | 46
The Butcher | 47
Alphabets | 49
Covering the Mirrors | 50
What Is Faith, After All | 51
Reflections on a Text, Ninth Century Spain | 52
Shmita or the Seven-Year Itch | 54
Watching Over the Body | 56

IV

The Autopsy, a Love Poem | 60
Big Sue | 62
Interior at Paddington | 63
Animal under the Clothes | 64
Benefits Supervisor Sleeping | 65
Evening in the Studio | 66
Girl with a Kitten | 67
Painter's Mother Resting III | 68
Queen Elizabeth II | 69

Painter's Mother IV | 70
Pomme d'Amour | 71
Something in the Water | 73

V

The Secret Life of Bridges | 76
Fire Season | 78
Admiral Nimitz | 79
What Is This Fear that Comes from Silence? | 80
On a Suburban Street | 81
The Motorbikes | 82
Bottle | 83
Playing *Skachi* in Siberia | 85
Stumbling onto the Stolpersteine Project, Berlin | 86
First Wife | 88
Nothing Left to Do | 89
Happyville | 90
Master Class | 91

Notes | 93

Glossary | 95

About the Author | 97

Acknowledgments

Grateful acknowledgment is made to the editors of the following journals in which poems in this collection first appeared, sometimes in different versions.

Atlanta Review: "Admiral Nimitz"
Arroyo Literary Review: "Something in the Water" and "What Really Happened"
Blue Lyra Review: "Because the Porchlight Flickered"
Catamaran: "The Equation" and "Because"
Cider Press Review: "Sentries"
Conclave: "Hollowed Fruit"
Cooweescoowee: "Animals under the Clothes"
Crab Orchard Review: "January: Wyoming Storm"
DMQ Review: "The Edge of Things"
Empirical: "What I'd Ban"
Faultline: "Because One and the Other" and "Into the Forest"
Harpur Palate: "Animal Time" and "The Bottle"
Hayden's Ferry Review: "Big Sue" and "The Secret Life of Bridges"
Ilanot Review: "This is Where We Stand"
Illuminations: "Even Now" and "When Least Expected"
Jewish Journal: "Alphabets"
Journal of Compressed Art: "The Day it Changed"
The MacGuffin: "Betrayal"

Memoir: "Flying Off the Page"
Meridian: "Again the Crows"
Mid-American Review: "The Autopsy, a Love Poem"
Minnesota Review: "Reflections on a Text, 9th Century Spain"
Miramar: "Dare"
Mudfish: "First Wife"
Nimrod: "Painter's Mother IV"
North American Review: "Fire Season"
Pembroke: "Coneflower"
Poet Lore: "Nothing Left to Do"
Prime Mincer: "John Bower, Biologist, Explains Bird Calls"
Rattle: "What is Faith After All"
Slipstream: "Let Rust Take Its Rightful Place" and "What Followed"
Tiferet: "On the Eve of Yom Kippur, I Listen to the Rachmaninoff Vespers"
Tikkun: "Black Hat," "The Butcher," and "Covering the Mirrors"
Valparaiso Poetry Review: "Benefits Supervisor Sleeping" and "Long Shadows"
Women in Judaism: "Speaking in Tongues"

"Speaking in Tongues" was reprinted in *Manifest West: Western Weird* (2015); "Animal Time" in *American Life in Poetry: Column 544* (2015); "Admiral Nimitz" in *American Life in Poetry* (2017); "Sentries" in *Cider Press Review, Best of Volume 16* (2015); "Predicting Weather" in *Prairie Gold: An Anthology of the American Heartland* (2014); "A Watched Pot" in *The Bloomsbury Anthology of Contemporary Jewish American Literature* (2013); "What I'd Ban" in *Best of Empirical* (2012); "On A Suburban Street" in *A Bird Black as the Sun: California Poets on Crows and Ravens* (2011).

Completion of this manuscript was made possible by a residency at Surel's Place, Boise, Idaho, for which I am deeply indebted. Thank you to the National Park Service and Homestead National Monument of America, Nebraska, and Hubbell

Trading Post, Arizona, where some of these poems were written. I am grateful to the Barbara Deming Memorial Fund, Inc./ Money for Women for a 2015 grant used to go to Germany and back to Russia. Appreciation to Buryatia State University, Ulan-Ude, Republic of Buryatia, Siberia, and to Elena Baiartueva and colleagues for your warm welcome in winter. Thank you to Polly Gannon, Elena Leibson and Efim Levertov in St. Petersburg whose belief sustains me. To David, Jacob, and Hannah Berezin and Colleen Grennan for everything. To Mercedes Lawry, Peggy Aylsworth Levine and Antoinette Jaccard. To Marsha de la O, Phil Taggart, and the Ventura poetry community. To Andrea Carter Brown whose sharp eyes made this work better. I am grateful to Yvette M. Brown for permission to use her painting for the cover. Deep appreciation to Barbara Smith-Mandell and Truman State University Press for this poetry home.

I

The Edge of Things

Always look
for the edge of things
                    to judge when to step off
                        when to turn away

  There is no taking back the knife
        which divided my finger from its anchor
                            Why decades later
    I am not to be trusted
around sharp objects
        Just look at divers
            not the raised fin they fear
   but the eye sizing them up, the teeth poised
in their soft bed
        ready to snap open, to wrestle flesh from bone

Sentries

If you believe in the power of ravens, this all may be true.
An ex-wife claims she knew when her former husband had died,
though she had not seen him for thirty years.

Some believe in premonition.

A pond. The kind undiscovered for years,
until a woman pulls aside willow branches, lifts twigs pointy
as witches' fingers from the water.
Stripping, she eases in as the surface parts for her.

There are places where seasons cease to exist.
Time marked by light and darkness.

Others surely knew of this pond, but did not warn her.

The moon was of no help.

She began to swim as if weightlessness were a kind of god
willing to forgive everything.
Then she saw black ribbons in the water: snakes
gliding from both banks like sentries.

Dare

The neighborhood kids didn't worry about danger.
Not while perched on the slope down to the creek,
mayonnaise jars poised, leaning far out to catch tadpoles.
Not while climbing reliable oaks to branches
fragile as bones, tightropes strung over the street.

Holding our breath, we whizzed by the witch's house on bikes,
wrought iron fence strangled by ivy, blinds hiding something
									terrible.
Boys taunted girls to unlock the gate latch,
march the path bordered by hemlock.
No one took up the challenge.

Later on my best friend's mother packed her kids and headed to
									Guyana.
Trapped in the undergrowth of Jonestown, the older brother
murdered a congressman on the tarmac.
Evaded the poisoned brew, but jailed for life.
We'd moved by then, but even before my friend called,
I'd read about it in the papers.

One of us died at eighteen in the Viet Nam jungle.
Back then we'd never heard of friendly fire.
I dare you to say it was only the times.

Coneflower

All day watching the coneflowers.
Their many incarnations: the pale purple
with its thin, drooping petals like an umbrella's
skeleton, abandoned in a doorway after a storm.
Its cousin, the prairie coneflower,
with a cap twice as long as wide.
So boastful with that bullet head, brown-black
like a Russian fur hat and a stem four feet tall.
Its yellow petals pull downward, as if
nature were playing a little joke, the way a
beautiful woman will have one flaw, a dark mole
that may or may not spoil everything.

Flying Off the Page

The crows fly off the page heading west
black and white as they must be, though in this book
they will never be allowed to land.

Is refuge sweeter for being confined to a patch of green
sandwiched between peeling paint and chipped bricks?

For weeks drama on a Moscow roof, its fence a tangle
of wrought iron vines and flowers.
Clusters of ill-tempered birds shifted on spindly legs,
fighters waiting to enter the ring.
Bullies, they'd squawk and thrash to prevent
sparrows and thrushes from landing.
We are not the only species to covet real estate.

Smaller birds better off seeking refuge
in the birch forests that ring the city.

After I had babies, I'd rise in the dark, sleepwalk
to their rooms to check their breathing.
People once believed the soul escaped the body at night

to return to heaven and had to be enticed back every morning.
And a sneeze, an omen of death, expelled the soul.
Only a blessing would prevent Satan from snatching it.

On another page, a woman in a summer dress
leans from a window; wind ruffles her collar.
Shoulders bare, arm extended as if to call back her lover.
There is one more thing she must say to him.

Animal Time

                  I do better in animal time,
a creeping dawn, slow ticking toward dusk.
In the middle of the day on the Nebraska prairie,
I'm unnerved by subdued sounds, as if listening
through water, even the high-pitched drone of the
cicadas faint; the blackbirds halfheartedly singing.
As newlyweds, my parents drove cross-country to
Death Valley, last leg of their escape from New York,
the thick soups of their immigrant mothers, generations
of superstitions that squeezed them from all sides.
They camped under stars that meant no harm.
It was the silence that alerted them to danger.
They climbed back into their tiny new car, locked
its doors and blinked their eyes until daylight.

Predicting Weather

Even Aristotle believed in earthquake weather:
   Tremors caused by winds trapped in caves,
air breaking the surface. Cloud formations.
   An earthly stillness. Unseasonable warmth. Calm.

Today before dawn, here in Nebraska, fists of hail,
   the windows shaking, then rain slapping in waves.
      Nothing unusual in these parts: thunder cursing,
the sky knocked about by lightning.

The first time the siren went off, I didn't know
   what it was: a burglar alarm,
      the water heater about to burst.
After the high-pitched wail, a man's firm but steady
voice announced (from where?):
   Severe weather. Tornado watch.

I suppose it's what you're used to. In Los Angeles
   when the glass shudders and rattles,
      I stand under a doorway,
   grab the animals to prevent their bolting.
   Even so, when the cupboard doors swing open
      and the crockery takes flight
there's a moment of stunned beauty
      before the crash of porcelain on tile.

Long Shadows

Before we understood suffering, we played a game:
    What sense would you prefer to lose?
I'd choose taste, glad to give up the bitter radishes I'd
push to the edge of my plate, a mound of ammunition
I wouldn't dare launch at my brother. I'd happily forego
the dark nuggets we guessed incorrectly were steak
when it was kidney in the pies served at school lunch.
The headmistress who paced with a ruler tapping
her palm, checking if we'd eaten our portions,
the sting to our hands when we had not: touch,
a code for punishment. Blindness
too frightening to contemplate, too
familiar, as my route home looped in front of
The School for the Blind, though rarely were children
out front, and never did they play sidewalk games.
I didn't know the many pregnancies
my mother had lost, the *blank* before my
brother's adoption, the *blank* after, followed
by my risky birth. And the one stillbirth.
Was it a boy? A girl? Did they name it?
Or did it join those other whispers about cousins
my family couldn't trace in Germany?
I'd give up hearing if it meant not catching
the worry in my parents' voices, give up
the smell of leaves burning, so as
not to be reminded of that other smoke.
So many secrets buried in the backyard.
Even after thinning, the trees tightened
in a circle, casting long shadows all night.

Hollowed Fruit

    Neither of us accepts defeat
though my position is slipping.
    Out before dawn hollowed fruit
swing like skulls from low-hanging
    branches of the orange tree.
For a long time I refused to admit the culprit.
    One night a silhouette crept
along the phone line, magnified.
    If I don't acknowledge it,
will the tree rat disappear?
    Sometimes the rope we cling to
starts to fray, our grip loosening.
    The man who believed in the humanity
of bears had it all wrong.
    Nature not to be trusted.
One morning the noxious vine of
    morning glory reached its tendrils
through the windowsill.
    The next day it had grown two inches.
A cockroach scurried across the kitchen counter.
    If I were superstitious, I'd know they
were omens.

What Followed

    The moon bore down lunging through the stars
No matter that the girl ducked into an alley,
darted in a shortcut through a park,
it followed her.

    Inside, she zipped open her wallet and
the moon bounced out, ricocheted from floor
to ceiling, off the earthquake-cracked walls.
She opened a window hoping it would fly.

    As the weeks slipped by, the moon shrank, the stars vanished.
She grew complacent. The moon masqueraded
as a harmless sliver. It hooked its nail
under her collar and yanked.

    There are people who crave all they see:
a woman falls for a man with such a smile that sucks her in.
Others tumble for a sweeping view over a valley.
She only wished to be left alone.

    But the moon, the stubborn moon,
grew bulbous again, blood red after a scorching day,
then yellow as discarded parchment.
Every time she looked up, it hung there, waiting.

The Equation

Consider the equation between poison and beauty:
Does each black stripe on a monarch butterfly add to its lethal
                                                                             potency?

Females with wings of Jerusalem gold, the males boasting
a deep rust with a black spot on their hind wings.
Do such gaudy colors attract or repel birds hunting a mouthful?

Heavenly plants are often the most poisonous:
angel's trumpet, the Easter lily a symbol of the Virgin Mary and
                                                                                      deadly.

In Victorian times each flower was assigned a meaning:
  Marigold = jealousy
  Lily of the valley = purity of heart, sprung from Eve's tears

A man I loved asked me to plant oleander; I refused, convinced
he would succumb to the curve of its petals, lick its white lips.

Later we walked through a meadow of clinging nettles,
dead-ending at a small pile of bones.
He did not notice the ducks lifting over the water.

Late January: Wyoming Storm

Where are the animals as the wind blows
the snow horizontally?
Can the hawk maintain its perch in the storm?
And did the trio of white-tailed deer
huddled off Lower Piney Creek survive?
Soon the wind will strip seedpods
from the spindly maple; the snow
will be lifted from the ground.
Dormant roots torn from the red soil.

This is the land of Genesis.
A sea formed, then vanished, a basin
filled with floors of sedimentary rock.
> *Let the waters below the sky be gathered*
> *Let the dry land appear.*

Sediment to rock, trilobites
in the sandstone and shale.
Minerals float to the surface, limestone
to marble. Pink-tinged granite,
there for the gathering.
You can track this landscape the way
a phrenologist traces protuberances of a skull.
Topography that expands, then
compresses to its vanishing point.

The wind so fierce this morning, the world
is being stripped back to nothingness.
First the roof will pull away.
Wrenching the house from its foundation
takes more effort, but even the stucco
will give way, at last returned
to the place of its birth by a creek bed.

II

Speaking in Tongues

    In unfamiliar landscapes
Yiddish diminutives, terms of endearment,
drop from my tongue, morsels, a little sweet, a little sour.

Then the curses begin their training: bulking up
on a diet of sarcasm and sneers, centuries of practice
honed to this art.

    The Wyoming cowboys in the bar
                    stare at me in disbelief.
They're used to horses that whinny but this sounds
like something you'd attach to those decorated manes,
the kind no real cowboy would get near.

A geologist, also not from these parts, explains in a tone
reserved for restless third graders, just how to find a vein of coal.
Never mind the tops of mountains sheared off crew-cut style.
If he doesn't find it, someone else will.

    In Virginia they asked if
I'd ever seen a real movie star. I've seen plenty:
without all that makeup, they're not so special.

Those cowboys really did tie bandanas around their necks;
you could tell they knew knotting from birth.
They didn't have to scuff their boots to show they meant business.

These curses didn't know where to go. The bar was full.
Every time one fiddler sat down, another jumped in.
Barely room to squeeze in between one slide of a bow and the next.
The windows fogged up; outside the snow thickened like insulation.
It was time to get serious: the curses hauled out everything they had and let them have it.

What Really Happened

      Time now to set the record straight.

    His car.   Hers.   A pedestrian.

The corner where the bystanders watched.

    Either noon or sometime later.

The driver's window fell in, glass slivers or a light rain.

    Or it exploded out, shards pinging on the door in Morse code.

Believe what you will. Each person, witness or participant,

      remembers differently. Two minutes replayed over years.

        Characters age; blame remains a constant.

The sun stayed in the sky uninvolved. Or it blinded everyone.

    The stains on the asphalt fading slower than you might think.

Contemplating Murder

She tried everything:

    1. giving it the evil eye
    2. an eviction notice
    3. tearing it limb from limb

but it ignored her efforts,
stubbornly sucking nutrients,
using night shadows as fortification.
Now over six feet tall, it towers
over her, daring her to violence.

        ◎ ◎ ◎

The clicking of a ballpoint pen
can drive you to distraction.
Or when the person next to you in Seat 15B
chews with his mouth open and
you have to close your eyes, say
a prayer that 93,000 lb.
of aluminum, titanium, plastics,
will lift off at all, when really you just want
to scream and tell him to shut his mouth.

        ◎ ◎ ◎

Do we really have to be grateful for small miracles?
Must we appreciate the unplanned for?

❀ ❀ ❀

She goes to Home Depot in disguise:
dark sunglasses,
cap low over the eyes.
No one would expect her on the poison aisle.
She slinks her way to check out,
paralyzed in line.
Will she go through with it or not?

Betrayal

                        My lungs are the new enemy,
    taunting me, puffed up
        like striped pantaloons on Swiss guards.
They used to be dependable,
        the slow in and out of breath,
    matching balloons slowing releasing air.
        No need to think about it.
Now in midsentence they squeeze shut, like the post office window
    when you've waited for forty-five minutes but
                it's lunchtime
      and the clerk slams the window down.
        Whose protection is the Plexiglass for anyway?
I've tried negotiating with my anatomy for a truce,
      an hour cough-free is not an unreasonable demand,
but that rascally pair know a good thing
        when they've got it and refuse to give.
They wait till the restaurant's bursting with patrons. I'm at a table
    with people I'm dying to impress—when a cough unleashes
            an explosion
so violent the diners scrape back their chairs and look for cover.
        They know a sick person when they hear it.
      Never mind my protestations. They feel the creep of
                      contagions.
Who they going to believe after all?
        This middle-aged woman or a pair of hoodlums
in matching dark suits, seductive smiles, pistols drawn.

Money Laundering

A black Mercedes sidles up beside a Georgian restaurant,
ever so slightly onto the sidewalk.
Even before the heavy doors swing open
you'd jump, if you happened to be walking by.

I have no experience in laundering money
but I got pretty good at spotting gangsters in Moscow.

The beauty supply store on Pico Blvd.
has an *Open* sign in the window but in the fifteen years
I've driven by, I've never seen anyone
going in or out.
Who would want to buy old hair dye anyway?
A perfect front, if you think about it.

Something unseemly about being
too interested in cosmetics or lotions,
though skin care is now highly
recommended for everyone.
Maybe it's generational.
I can pick out men with dyed hair
a mile away: too dark. They're always
so pleased with themselves.

Are drugs traded in the back room?
Cardboard boxes with bottles of shampoo
standing straight as foot soldiers.

Hundred dollar bills crammed into the corners.
A back door exiting into the alley.
Am I the only one to notice?

Maybe I'll stop at the police station
on my way home from class.
Got to be a big reward once I tell them.
I hope they let me come along.
I love sirens. I want to be the last push
to bust open that door.

Into the Forest

    No witch beckoned hither with a chicken bone finger,
though after two hours in the forest clearly lost,
it would not have been a surprise, at least to the wife,
if a house bricked with peppermints rose up from the junipers.

Instead they looped through redwoods so high the sky shrunk
to rectangles of pale light.

    The map was wrong, he said; she blamed herself,
always leaving the navigation to him, while she made lunches,
packed the car. An hour north their daughter in surgery.
A brief walk the treat they allowed themselves en route.

    There is a moment in every marriage when one partner looks
at the other as if for the first time.

Humor

> *After God made the world, he filled it with people.*
> *He sent off an angel with two sacks, one full of*
> *wisdom and one full of foolishness.*
>
> —from a Chelm story

When the angel flew overhead,
he forgot to bestow humor.
It's been a handicap all my life.
Even in my own language I never understand jokes.
When I try to tell one, I forget the punch line.

Once a boy took me to see a stand-up comedian.
My date's face turned red as a balloon.
On the verge of popping, he was laughing so hard.
I tried not to look clueless, but it was obvious.
He never called again.

I used to think I was related to my children.
Once a year when the three travel from different corners
of the country and reconfigure on the couch,
they like to watch the late-night comedians.
At first I would ask questions, hoping to join in,
but it was clear I didn't belong.

A man I knew could command one eyebrow to dance.
Fat as a caterpillar, it would waken in a slight rumble,
then wriggle its way up, hovering there.
He was on to something; I'm sure of it.

Because One and the Other

Because one letter was never received
and the other never sent

Because the orange tree was swallowed
under a netting of white flies

The rose bush attacked by rust
that left its leaves a strange shining in the dark

The husband always on the left side of the couch
the wife shrunken to the right

Bruised boxers to opposite corners of the ring
They retreat to separate bedrooms

The conversation innocuous next morning
as if this were an improvement

After the husband leaves for work the wife
searches for the door with the polished handle
that if unpolished would turn dark as iron

What I'd Ban

If I were queen of the world,
dictator, minister of culture, I'd ban the phrase
At the end of the day, especially this election season
with the endless whine of interviews.

My husband vows to prohibit golf, but what's
so bad about it, other than the dumb outfits?
Middle-aged men should stay away from shorts
that turn knees into the knobs of walking sticks.

I despise purposeful misspellings.
Do you really gain anything by dropping a letter?
Light to *lite* or night to *nite*?

I'm starting to sound like Andy Rooney now, but thick
as my hair is, I'll never match those eyebrows.
When Rooney'd get really annoyed, they'd start to twitch,
twin propellers warming up on a prop plane.
Or a pair of moths about to swoop in tandem
to attack a tree dripping with ripe peaches.

The Dog Show

We are not dog people.
Late nights we sit at our desks,
backs to one another,
a cat on each lap.
So I cannot say what sucked
us into watching the Westminster
Kennel Club Dog Show on TV for hours.
The camera glued on owners' legs
in ballet flats (mostly chunky women),
trotting in circles past the judges.
Such variety of dogs: the car wash dog
(as the announcer named it), with its grey fur
swishing like the rags that slap
windshields. The Great Dane pulling
its owner until she seemed to plane over water.
It's true we each had our favorites.
Predictably I rooted for the unlikely pooches,
a sad-sack basset hound who looked miserable
but made it to the last round.
He chose a Scottish terrier whose fur
swept the floor as he scrambled to keep up.
Maybe that's why we stayed to the end,
wishing for once the little guy
could come out on top.
The difference between us:
I don't buy lottery tickets.
(I know I'll never win.)
He does; today could be his lucky day.

John Bower, Biologist, Explains Bird Calls

The birds here on Sehome Hill differ from those
in Seattle, ninety miles south; a kind of dialect he says in a
voice so patient you'd think he was explaining the obvious.
Say the birds meet between the two cities, some would
mingle, a few might mate, though many females
would refuse the advances, despite coaxing.

      Is it a kind of snobbery? The way my mother-in-law,
Boston-bred, looked down on the New Yorkers, as if
they'd just tumbled out of steerage, as her own parents had,
in fact, their leather suitcase shoved under the bunks,
squeezed shut with a rope that frayed all across the Atlantic.

      The way she looked down on that New York accent,
be it tinged with a brogue or weighted down by a folksy Yiddish.
It's the difference between the snide call of a mockingbird and
the trill of a Townsend warbler: This one from the right side of
                                                                      the tracks,
the mocker not. Even a mountain range can make a difference:
remember the Valley girl accent everyone imitated in the 70s?

      High up a bushtit nest hangs, its shape a sock,
brown, bits sticking out, either art or lack of attention to detail.
What will the birds eat? No salmonberries yet,
the coldest spring on record, though the birds' migration north
                                                                                     unabated.

*Listen there, that one's a male late in spring without a mate.
He's showing off, just in case a female, even an old one, will have him.
Little chance now, but he's full-throated, trying not to show his desperation.*

Let Rust Take Its Rightful Place

When fever invades the body like a dybbuk do not attempt to
                              expel it with psalms

    The border between grace and acquiescence is porous

Let rust take its rightful place

    Rain not be ashamed of tearing branches from their mooring

First windows chatter in their frames then the earthquake catapults

    cups and dishes into the hemisphere

    The night the tornado warning sounded, wind snaked
                                through the walls

Clouds pressed down like a lathe   the rain grew fat as worms

This Is Where We Stand

The problem is corners.
      We believed them trustworthy
   but how easily a door rips from its hinges
              in a storm, then hangs
incapable of righting itself
    a tongue from the mouth of a dog
      And symmetry!
              A myth that balance prevails
  Look at your mother's photo
            Note the left eye, bigger as if the right
had been caught in a twitch
    or a squint in the blare of afternoon sun
           She did not want to stand there
  See her left hip jutted out, angry

No wonder the yellow caution tape wraps around the front of the
                                                            house
    damaged by earthquake: danger

Because the Porch Light Flickered

Because the porch light flickered
the moths circled first one way, then the other,
thrown off their habitual trance.

We watched the clouds
dependent on them for predictions:
Would the storm hit or bypass us altogether?

What passes for seasons here:
the towering Australian oak exploding in full leaf
when the other trees are shedding.

Searing heat on Rosh Hashanah.
We secretly plead with Abraham not to strike Isaac,
for God to give a last minute reprieve or failing that,

to suspend Abraham's arm midair. One slip
of our attention and the story could rewrite itself
in a bloodbath, certainty lost before another sundown.

Faith and doubt jockey for position, the way
a marathoner sizes up the competition before
planting her feet in the front line.

Will her finishing time be dependent
on always wearing the same red shorts?
Or closing her eyes before the starting gun goes off?

Everyone throws salt over the left shoulder,
but how many of us blind the devil
so he can't witness our misdeeds?

In the Middle Ages left-handed people
were burned at the stake.
I'm Jewish, so doubly cursed.

Starting on a journey with your right foot
is good luck, while if your left foot itches,
your travels will end in sorrow.

III

Because

Because I cannot leave this body
    I dream I am flying

The air splits   subdivides
    splinters into layers of grey and worn lavender

Voices penetrate as if through fog
    in languages perhaps I never knew

No wonder men choose to be ghosts
    Switch the door from one wall to another

Women no more fragile though a wandering
    hand to the cheek can betray

I return to the monastery in the Pushkin Hills
    the chapel now silent though I fear exposure

Candles bleed light and shadow onto
    cracked icons peering through silver

A young woman sloshes a bucket of water
    her braid a metronome swinging on her spine

Monks with dark beards hurry past
    as if God records how many hours of service

Because I cannot leave this body
   I climb a circular staircase to the bell tower

Black Hat

The black hat. The wig. The shawl. The thick stockings. The kerchief. The skullcap. The hidden fringes. The posted decrees. Neighbors spitting with suspicion. Roaring hooves. Thwack of sabers. The night escape. The ship. Stacked bunks in steerage. The stench. The elderly. Time peeling. The deck. The railing. The jolt of docking. Gulps of fresh air. Shoving. The brick buildings. Family clusters. The names noted: last, first. Lost syllables. Truncated. Neutered. New name assigned. Whispers down the shuffling line. Questions dangling in stagnant air. Men with clipboards. Lifted shirts. Stethoscope on bare skin. Prodding for fever, rashes. Pinpoint of light in the eyes. Men in uniform. A limp. Stifled coughs. Girl yanked out of line. The shiny badge. The rejected. The separation. The chain-link fence. The black hat.

Even Now

1.

I am afraid of rubber toys, their molded flesh unlike our
                                                                          impermanence
Their squeaks what our voices will be reduced to

2.

An old scrub oak hollowed by fire refuses to succumb to the
                                                          drought this non-winter
The sea of grasses around it stripped of greens and blues

3.

The bus's lace curtains could not mask the smell of killings
                                                              sixty-five years ago
A sleek cube in a birch forest, monument to the slaughtered Jews
                                                              of northwest Russia
The bus does not stop

4.

My grandparents never looked back
They had no choice but to go forward

5.

I am pulled back as if by electrical current to a country that will
                                                              always hate my kind
Even now, years away, the words circulate, jab in the ribs when I
                                            get too comfortable where I am

A Watched Pot

How many years waiting?
So many pots to remember: a blue enamel chipped
around its rim perched in a tiny room in Athens.
A teakettle that lost its whistle in Rome.
The many kitchens of my childhood.
My father was an itinerant do-gooder.
He gave up on religion but memorized
the dictum to repair the world.
As refugees poured out of Europe,
we sailed the other way on a three-decked ship
out of New York Harbor.
A trunk with leather straps
that tattered over the years.
I was what they called a sickly child,
feverish with coughs that shivered
through my small frame.
My mother wiped down surfaces
morning to night to kill off the microbes
waiting to leap into my lungs.
She abandoned the superstitions of her parents:
spitting over a shoulder to ward off the evil eye,
never boasting about her children.
Science, she believed in, and cleanliness.
The water boiled extra long.
I caught the restlessness of my father,
bundling my own three children for a flight
that bumped its way from Los Angeles to Frankfurt,
Warsaw to St. Petersburg.
Their own lungs scarred and shredded by asthma.

We were warned of the water, parasites
from the canals in the rusted pipes.
I bought a timer and stood guard over the stove.
When the Russian government shut off the hot water
to clean the city's pipes, out came vats to boil water
for the bath, for the tub to wash our clothes.
It is now January in California.
I would like a cup of hot tea.
How easy it all is, a polished teakettle,
the filtered water ready to boil in a minute's time.

Again the Crows

Summoned outside by squawking.
The skeleton oak fills with crows in the top branches.
Black flames against the early sky,
this Sunday before Christmas.
Just yesterday, huddled in an unheated shul, we listened to
the chanting of the Torah, the burning bush that would not be
                                                consumed.
Even a lowly thornbush is irreplaceable.
Moses argued with the voice, but finally could not deny it.
If only such signs could be believed.
I see them everywhere.

The Day It Changed

The stair shifted as she stepped on it
                sliding to the right then left

        She accepted this without question, the way a woman
                              accommodates
           the next person crowding into the subway car
                        before the doors slam

The stair untethered from its brethren above and below hovered

                You don't believe this but it's true

                      ✺ ✺ ✺

        The bluebird harangued for a week: judge, jury,
                                    sentence meted out
Without defense or recourse she stood before the orange tree
                              bowing her head

     Then visitations   men   women
          Some had wings sprouting from their shoulder blades
Small children sang wordless melodies

        She grew afraid to mount any staircase or ladder

certain a rung would fly into her hand   a staff to shake at God
          If she threw it down water would spout

              There would be no turning back

On the Eve of Yom Kippur,
I Listen to the Rachmaninoff Vespers

Is every portal to heaven equal?

    These ten days when the book of life lies open
before the pages flutter shut

    The reeds are on both sides of the river
        but the choices not always ours to make:
to cross or not
    to remain where we are or chance fleeing

An uneasy marriage of expectation and guilt
    So many temptations to succumb to

    Once in Novgorod I stumbled into a funeral service

All I intended was to gaze at the cathedral's stained glass windows

    The Orthodox priest swung the censer toward the
        congregation   Though
I was standing in the back, he caught my eye and knew I did
    not belong

    Now on the eve of this Jewish holiday

I listen to the Rachmaninoff vespers and when I look up

    the windows have blurred into waves of blue and gold
        darkened by centuries of incense

The Butcher

Yonatan ben Yosef, Jonathan, son of Joseph,
was a *shochet*, a butcher, in the Pale of Settlement.
With a smooth blade, he slit the throats of steers,
drained the blood into a bucket, salted the meat
to make it fully kosher.

He didn't own the cattle, only slaughtered it.
Shtetl life was brutal, the threat of pogroms constant.
I know only that and the eyes that pierce the photo
on my mantle, so savage my children took it down
and buried it in a cupboard.

Maybe those eyes blackened when his son was conscripted
into the tsar's army, landing in a Cossack unit.
A scrawny Jew with a caterpillar moustache,
who couldn't match the sabers or vodka of his fellow soldiers.

Six years later, he slipped out of the army, walked to a train,
a boat to cross the ocean. This must be the wandering gene
that propelled my father to leave the comforts of America
to help rebuild Europe and later flung me afield to Russia
with my own children.

Now in Nebraska, I think of these men buried on both coasts,
far from this center of the country. The prairie stores
its own sad histories: winters that smothered the hopes
of homesteaders, plagues that devoured the crops,
dust storms that darkened the skies.

This morning, after the thunder has crumpled to a whimper and the rain quiets, the chant of the red-winged blackbird bounces from green ash to red cedar and the partridge pea flaunts its yellow. It is impossible to remain gloomy, even for this granddaughter of immigrants fed on mistrust and shadows.

Alphabets

Believe in the alchemy of letters
        but never in their permanence.

  Just look how the *aleph* was stripped of its
rightly earned place to begin the Torah
        how the *bet* is sheltered—
but only on three sides
        so its wind tunnel thrusts the reader forward.

    In Russian the silent letters gather in the cheek like
magic pebbles waiting to drop from the tongue. And the chutzpah

of English, its misleading spelling. Tell me, how can anyone
        ever learn it?

I have returned to America, but my dreams are a kite whose tail is
    strung with
  alphabets of all these languages and when I awaken

to the Morse code of birds in the oak tree I do not know
        how to translate this into prayer.

Covering the Mirrors

After a funeral, they were covered with black cloth,
some draped with shawls like a scalloped valance.
Leftover sewing scraps, wool, linen, synthetic,
anything to shroud the odd-shaped mirrors,
though sometimes a corner was exposed like a woman
whose ankle peeks forbidden from under a long skirt.

A mourner must shun vanity during *shiva*, focusing inward
but as a child I wondered if this were to avoid ghosts,
for don't the dead take their time leaving?
I'm of a generation where grandparents disappeared,
great aunts with European accents,
rarely an explanation provided to us children.

My mother died too young.
With a baby in arms I couldn't bear to fling
that dark cloth over the glass.
After all she had come back from the dead so often,
even the doctors could not explain it.
Each time I looked in a mirror my mother gazed back.
I could never tell if she were trying to tell me something
or to take the baby with her.

What Is Faith, After All

At ten, newly returned from living in England,
I sat in a rabbi's study reading about a vicar's daughter.
When he asked about the novel in my lap, I stammered,
mortified at being caught reading about another religion.
As if faith were so fragile I'd make the switch just like that.
A traitor revealed.

Thirty years later, leaving Russia, my elderly friend
made the sign of the cross over me, as I backed down
the dark staircase, tearful we'd never see each other again.
My religion irrelevant; her protection what mattered.
But didn't my grandfather trek across Russia's broad back

to flee Cossack sabers blessed by this sign and Orthodox priests
sprinkling holy water on soldiers bound for pogroms?

That same trip, a friend in Novgorod gave me an icon
for safe travels back to America. I tucked it in my suitcase,
unsure if it would protect or doom me.

This act of betrayal could pull down the belly of the plane.

Now on the computer a writer talks about his newfound faith.
My husband walks in; my cheeks burn with betrayal, the red
snaking down my neck, my body, as if by listening I am signing
on and that man in sandals and dusty robes will enter and snatch
                                                                      me forever.

Reflections on a Text, Ninth Century, Spain

Sitting in a synagogue basement, we study a text over a thousand
                      years old by Rabbi Joseph ibn Abitur:
   Rules on a woman's right to exit a marriage
   If the husband torments her—without cause—should she receive
                                          severance?

To debate a word like *hikkah* "strike, hit" ranging from slapping
                          (once) to beating (repeatedly)

That slippery: *without cause.*

My neighbor berated his wife in front of us: a meal undercooked,
                          a grad school paper put off.
Even the more serious—his betrayal, a baby dying, her fault.

   Must there always be an explanation for an unraveling?

My parents' friend walked out on her marriage in 1963, leaving
                          three young daughters.
Such beautiful children, my mother said, by way of condemnation,
                                              a scandal.

   Who can say what goes on behind closed doors?

This woman traded a view from Coit Tower for a Jerusalem sun
                        that brought warmth but not solace.
She struggled in a language that did not slide easily from her tongue.

Upon marriage a Jewish groom is obliged to pay the bride a fixed
amount should divorce occur.

The council of rabbis has the power to rule.

*Do we hold him to giving a writ of divorce,
or do we hold her to dwelling with her husband?* ibn Abitur asked.

More than one kind of strangulation.

Shmita or the Seven-Year Itch

        Leave it to the Jews to choose the unbalanced:
Seven can never add up: four rocks in one fist, three in another
    No will to throw them

Zeus never grasped more than one thunderbolt in each hand
                           He trusted his own power

    Gad, the Hebrew word for fortune, equals seven
        The seven laws of Noah: six are negative commands
Add to the three patriarchs the four women: Leah, Rachel,
                               Rebecca and Rivka
  to reach the same off-kilter number

Joseph prophesized seven years of plenty, followed by seven of
                                  famine
      Who can forget the illustrations of childhood books?
  Those poor cows with ribs so prominent we dared one
                            another to count them

      At her wedding the bride circles the groom seven times
After a person's death, the family sits on low stools for seven
                             days of mourning

This is the year of *Shmita*, the seventh year when Jews must not:
                    plow or plant, prune or harvest

Leave the land fallow, invite the stranger to pick
                              apples strung from
branches, to gather wheat from resting fields

Joshua marched the Israelites seven times around the walls of
                              Jericho and, as the song goes,
The walls came tumbling down

Watching Over the Body

    When my father lay dying in the hospital
I decided to go home for an hour or so. The children
young, I did not want to leave them long.

    Before I entered again, I stood
in the doorway afraid to hear bad news.
A floater nurse said she brought her lunch in,

    ate it on her lap so my father would not
be alone, though his eyes remained closed,
his breathing a rattle of pebbles.

    She asked my forgiveness for this act,
when it should have been the opposite, she who did
not know him, but did not want to leave him.

    In some Jewish households, after
a person dies, a man watches over the body
all night, reciting *Tehillim,* Psalms.

    Now I am on Navajo lands
where ghost sickness can spread to the living
if the body is not given a proper burial.

    Each night my father visits,
a version of himself from before I was born,
a camp counselor in the Catskills,

a young man about to leave
the tenement of his childhood for a land
of redwoods, pines and promise.

IV

The Autopsy, a Love Poem

What did the surgeons think when they first opened the body,
saw the tight-fisted heart crouching beneath a fan of ribs?

A spleen that threatened to unleash its venom,
the muscles of an arm flexed to show its strength?

In ancient cultures, a man who became disfigured, even dying
to protect his children, could not enter the afterlife.

After a mother dies, can she watch her children stumble
through adolescence before she lets go? How is the soul

tethered to the body? The first night, as you slept, the light
shifted from slate to an uncertain gray, as if it too were waiting

for a prophecy. Its own worst enemy, it sends fatty stock cars
chugging through veins or tricks hormones to swagger like teenagers.

Is it irresponsible in middle age to give in to desire
when the spine has already been unzipped so many times?

Stones bind us to our past, yours Jerusalem the gold, mine
the crumbling palaces of St. Petersburg, each of us with siblings

cut down young—as if we could have rescued them, bargained
to save their broken bodies, traded our own futures.

Before the sixteenth century no official autopsies had ever been done. In *The Anatomy Lesson of Dr. Tulp* the corpse appears lit within, spotlighting the faces of the guild members that hover over it; their concentration spills back over the body; knowledge perhaps, not love, the key to immortality.

Big Sue

we call her and it's no wonder why. But how she can sleep
while his eyes rake her figure, then fling her image onto canvas?
Her hand cradles a breast that resembles not flesh exactly,
mysterious as the mound I stumbled on one cold spring in
                                                                       County Sligo.

She dreams on a couch the painter bought for her, a deep
seat to accommodate the body that spreads where it can.
Stuffing oozes from the sofa's arms, grey and dirty white cotton.
Leaves sprout in a pattern of clotted vines, faded roses.
The stems of her own sturdy legs curl slightly.
Gobs of paint, thick whorls of it.
Her brow knots, as if to free itself from the confines of her form.

She is asleep and naked all these years, even after the painter has died.
I want to be that at home
in the house of my body.
Instead I examine its shelves and folds, check for new decay,
how it ages more under my stare.

Interior at Paddington

    The man in the painting
will die young because a cigarette hangs
permanently between his second and third fingers.
But in fact Harry Diamond lived to eighty-five.

He stands in an I-dare-you gangster pose,
though you might recognize this mirror image by Holbein:
full-length portraits of Henry VIII so real
rubies and emeralds could almost be plucked
from his fat fingers and folds of velvet.
No fur trimming here, just a grubby open mackintosh,
making the figure appear even smaller than normal.

    Instead of clutching gloves,
as royalty would, Harry's right fist is clenched,
palm up, nicotine stained. He stares at a potted palm
as if sizing up an opponent. A flick of the wrist and
he'd throw a fast one to the jaw, the jaunty curl sprouting
upright from his head notwithstanding.
Those oversized glasses might be a disadvantage
his opponent could use.

That character leaning against an outside wall,
probably an adversary waiting to ambush Harry.

The rug needs straightening, couldn't he see that?
Its red, the color of faded blood that will never wipe clean.

Animal under the Clothes

Man and dog sprawl on a bed,
their relationship unclear.
What love passes between them?

The man does not age in the painting
nor blink, his solid stare off to the side,
head thrust back, barely on the bed,
arm under and across the dog.

These are the basics, a room devoid of color.

His thoughts drift to later when he will meet friends,
talk about his irrational boss, those small
complaints that consume us.

The dog will die some years later,
but on this day, poised for the painter,
they lie as if nothing else matters,
as if they will always be this young,
this muscular, legs twitching
for the long run, oblivious
of the scars that await them.

Benefits Supervisor Sleeping

Even on the canvas, the skin breathes, as dough rises
and falls without visible help.
I wonder how she could sleep when the painter was studying her.
One arm supports a breast that resembles not flesh
exactly, but a mound, unknowable as Medb's Cairn
atop a sheep path in County Sligo.

He bought that couch for her, a deep seat, ample enough
for her body, patterned with roses and haphazard vines,
stuffing poking out.
The journalist asks if it were not a bit daunting to have one's
generous breasts and lolling stomach revealed.
Big Sue laughs; she was nervous at first, but got used to it.

In college I spent a year figure drawing in a room with corner
                                                                         windows.
One model was beautiful, perfectly rounded,
with an ease many women would envy, never
flinching under our concentrated gaze.
She banked her beauty. I cannot think of any woman
who trusts her body with such certainty.
We are all too ready to pick at the parts, thighs spilling out,
eyes set too close, ankles thick as winter stockings.
The Benefits Supervisor is still sleeping after all these years,
a comfort that she never ages, no fresh wrinkles to examine.
No peering in the mirror wondering whom she had become.

Evening in the Studio

Who can forget *Queen Elizabeth II*, frowning, cheeks
$\qquad\qquad\qquad\qquad\qquad$ unnaturally pale,
lips pursed in annoyance; two question marks on her forehead.

Roadmap streaks on the face of the *Woman in the White Shirt*,
alleyways coming to dead ends, forks in the road above her eyes.

$\quad$ Of course there were other portraits before "Big Sue."

$\quad$ But in *Evening in the Studio*, she sprawls
on the floorboards, blood smudged on her breasts and thighs,

while behind her, a young woman tucked in a rocking chair with
a flowered throw, ignores the reek of violence in front of her.

I want paint to work as flesh, he said.

Sometimes the body does not want to be told what to do:
$\quad$ it collapses, petals open.

$\quad$ Big Sue was not ashamed. The mound of her stomach a cairn.
Breasts boulders, matching guards at the head of the tomb.

I look on hungrily. Turn away.
$\quad$ Think about my own body.

Flesh collapsing in middle age,
$\quad$ addicted to the bottle of dye.

$\qquad$ Will we ever be as brave?

Girl with a Kitten

Visitors stare hard then quickly look away.
Those large, glassy, almond-shaped eyes
could turn on us.
Accusatory. Who would not believe her?

Face flat, unbearably white, expression imperious.
It seems impossible that she should not be trembling
one critic said.
She holds the kitten around the neck.
Resigned, it stays perfectly still.
She could so easily squeeze the life out of it.

What life is there in this portrait?
The small frizz of her otherwise flat hair
sprouts like capillaries.
Her jacket pale as a shroud.
No wonder her marriage to Lucian did not last.
How could it?

Painter's Mother Resting III

Save the intimacy of intertwined paisleys
with their jaunty fishtails patterned on her dress,
no sentiment in this portrait.
She lies on her back, a fierce stare into
the distance, unwilling to concede anything.
Grey hair thinning. Broken capillaries on
her cheek raked by the back of the paintbrush.
One arm bent at her shoulder, hand facing up;
the other on her stomach, fingers slightly curled
under, wedding band on her right hand.
How long has she lain there, stillness dictated
by the painter or her own flood of memories,
Lucian young, her husband still living?
Now the sheet grey, pillow discolored, indented,
age pushing her onward.

Queen Elizabeth II

No one can blame him for his honesty.
Hadn't the painter already shown male genitalia front on
and Big Sue sprawling recklessly, flesh drooped over a sofa?
He said this commission was like a polar expedition.

In the posing photo, she sits on a wooden chair, a small woman,
compact, hands on her lap. She eyes the painter warily.
Her taste leans to still lifes, not the aggressive portraits
of this painter, but again, she succumbs to duty.
Scrutinized many times, her love for her corgis,
millions spent on upkeep of her castles.
She never chose this position, the curse of genetics.

The critics lined up even before the paint dried,
"You're no oil painting, Ma'am," the *Mirror's* headline screamed.
(Tabloid outrage manufactured.)
His unsparing approach not a secret.
The queen stripped of elegance. Even with broad strokes,
lips tight, slight boredom in her opaque eyes.
A pair of Rorschach question marks on her forehead,
neck broad as a rugby player's.

820 portraits of her, this not the worst and at 75
she knew to nod and smile graciously.
What seethes beneath the coils and spins of paint?
What transpired between this queen who masks her emotions
and a painter who flings his own onto canvas remains a secret.

Painter's Mother IV

      stares at an unseen object
perhaps on a table just out of reach.
A slight frown gathers between brows raised quizzically.

      She is old and cannot understand why
she is a suitable subject for portraiture, but this is not the first
question she does not ask her son.

      Her hair loosely tied back, rebellious strands escape,
falling behind her neck, her torso covered by a sweater that leaks
brown onto her jaw line and the pockets of her cheeks.

      Is it resignation or impatience that has thrust her
onto this chair in front of a background swathed in more brown
                                        and a stripe of grey?
After all she has put up with, she deserves color,

a red flower splotched on a lapel, a gnarl of purple yarn to
                                          occupy her hands.
But this is what they do to old people, forcing them to pull a
                                          chair to a window
as if any view will satisfy.

Pomme d'Amour

In 1600 Europe, when a man bit into a tomato, it was a death wish.
All knew of its poison, how it seeped into the bloodstream,
red mixing with red. They watched for signs: the man's eyes
to roll back in his head, froth to spill over his swollen lips.
The pewter did it, tomato acid causing the lead to leach into food.
The poor eating on wooden plates did not have this problem.
For once poverty had its uses.

Two centuries later, 1820 to be exact,
Colonel Robert Gibbon Johnson stood on the steps
of a New Jersey courthouse to eat a tomato.
Was he being paid for these antics?
Did a circle of friends support him, holding a blanket
soft as moss in case he fell?
No one doubted this fruit, this vegetable was poisonous.
Beer sold to quench the townspeople gathered to jeer him.

Decades after the poison myth, the French believed
in *pomme d'amour* as aphrodisiac, its juice slut-red,
the first bite pure passion.
Succulent, ripe, the other forbidden fruit.
Catholics questioned its morality, earning a place
on the brethren's list of forbidden dishes: naked on the vine,
a scarlet temptation to lust-filled young men, powerless
to resist, while the leaves, rubbed between fingers, toxic.
The plant, a cousin of nightshade.

In a cracked bowl on a wooden table, summer's
first tomatoes nestle between two peaches,
surrounded by pears ripening.
Some swear by early fruit, the bursting juice of a new season.
Others believe Indian summer best, just before the fall chill.
The garden today gloomy with the gray of beach fog,
but the kitchen voluptuous with possibility.

Something in the Water

—after a Flemish painting

 The hooded executioner stepped
from a painting in my childhood straight into
a recurring dream, pushing aside the lush grass
 and the peasant's billowing sleeves

The raised scythe of that executioner follows me
back and forth across the ocean

 Padlocks on rusted boxes spring open
The secrets stored inside ooze out, poisoning
even the safest of marriages

 Something in the water caught my eye:
a gleaming fin, head of a seal, perhaps a surfer
I couldn't tell, but knew enough not to let my eye linger
for that patch of clinging road has brought down many cars

 Next morning afraid I'd read of a surfer pulled under

If I could push the shape back that December morning

The world spins past and we are powerless
to stop the wrenching of limbs

V

The Secret Lives of Bridges

1.

Words drift through the grating like ash, torn scraps of paper

>*He proposed* says a voice cracking
>the sure steps of women crossing

Later an elderly couple shuffles from one side to the other
>Whispers detached from the meaning of words

These two see into the future, peer into the long stretch of
>>>darkness ahead

2.

These rooms hidden beneath the Brooklyn Bridge

>Tell me your secrets

When city workers inspecting the bridge pried open the vault
>what bounty:

water drums, metal canisters of crackers
>352,000 of them   still edible it seems

To step inside: this history. Civil defense agencies barbed-wire
>barriers that hugged
>>the bridge in the Korean War

The squatting under desks in my childhood Khrushchev
>pounding his shoe
>>We did as we were told   Did we believe it would protect us?

It was about being saved
Brooklyn my family's refuge from a war about to crack open
My grandparents had already given up everything
What more could be asked

Fire Season

Fracked oil bubbles up and floods the leafy streets of
Marshall, Michigan, a town with robber baron houses
blue and yellow. The meandering path I wandered
beside the Kalamazoo River now underwater.

Further north, an early May blizzard in Minnesota
smothers roofs as people press against front windows
stunned by the freakish snow, seeking explanation.

It's true I come by my superstitions naturally,
a stroller not purchased before the baby's birth,
a *hamsa* in the crib to ward off the evil eye.
Kinehora, the children should be healthy.
One can never be too careful.

Watching local news today, the fire tightens its noose around
                                                          Los Angeles.
Scrub oak already brown, foothills parched.
The flames appear as letters, words break apart,
fling to opposite hillsides, throwing curses in many languages.

Admiral Nimitz

Every day in summer I'd cross the border;
he'd nod, pick up the horseshoes,
hand me one, triple the size
of my palm, and say, *You first*. We'd play
away the afternoon. Few words
punctuated the clank of horseshoe
against stake, until the fog rolled in
and I'd retrace my steps home.
I was five or six; he, white-haired,
however old that meant.

One evening my father sat me down,
spoke in the exaggerated tone
adults adapt for children, asked
if I knew who *he* was.
Admiral Nimitz, of course, though
I knew nothing of his command
of the Pacific Fleet and was less impressed
than if he'd landed a horseshoe.

He was a calm man, a useful attribute
for sending young men to their deaths.
The only time I saw him upset,
raccoons had invaded from their hideouts
in the hills, attacked the goldfish in his pond,
leaving muddy footprints as they escaped.
As far as I knew, this was his only defeat.

What Is This Fear that Comes from Silence?

Swamped by sirens, leaf blowers, the incessant honking of
impatient drivers in the city, I have escaped,
only to feel the discomfort of space and quiet.
A coyote tears through the trash
after the hens are locked up for the night.
The ravens swoop for rabbits chewing on the wet grass.
I do not need to hear these to know
to be afraid.

            * * *

Through the thick walls of the hogan
a chorus of insects seeps in: strings of cicadas,
brass of crickets, a base line I cannot identify.
Sleep snatched away by the thrumming.

            * * *

Driving yesterday for hours on an isolated highway.
As the clouds threw shadows onto the far hills,
the brown-red slopes darkened to dried blood.
A cry rose in my throat though no sound emerged.
Unsure of my direction, no other cars in sight,
I knew the car would break down, night squeeze in.
No one would rescue me.

On a Suburban Street

The snake lay across the threshold
pretending it was nothing but a snake.
The rest of that day the hours broke
off in chunks, scattering into the scrub,
drifting back as the light shifted.
Next morning a spider crawled
from the stainless steel drain.
One pair of legs raised like scepters.
He declared the kitchen his,
dared me to turn on the faucet.
Then the crows returned.
A Greek chorus, black-hooded on the front lawn.
No scolding caws, just the pierce of accusation.
Nothing had changed.
And yet a divide between silence and noise.
In the backyard squirrels scampered up
the orange tree, burned out lanterns
of hollowed fruit in their wake.
The mockingbirds and warblers taunted,
bluebirds shrieked.
Along the street violet-tinged feathers wove
into a fence, rising and falling in the breeze.
Guarding the house from the evil eye
or a warning sign to others?
The sidewalk heaved from tree roots,
its lip split from an earthquake.
At dusk machine gun rumble: *caw-caw-caw.*
The heads of the crows bobbing as they reload.

The Motorbikes

multiply as the hours wear on,
at first harmless as a field at dawn
but later a battle between scooter and pedestrian
epic as the one between white larvae and farmer
now raging across Nebraska and Iowa.
As Americans, we believe ourselves resourceful,
ready to face the enemy and defeat him.
After all, what is this tiny wriggling body to us?
But the corn rootworm has its own arsenal,
waiting underground, mutating to vanquish our genetic tricks.
We become aware of its power when a windstorm flattens
the corn because the stalks were gnawed through at their base.
A scientist tests the soil, driving out larvae with hot, bright lights.
The larvae squirm, trying to escape the heat like the scooter
now making a figure eight between cars and people
on this wide Beijing boulevard.
This afternoon, the motorbikes swarm like gnats.
Only because I was pulled to safety can I tell you this.
The Angel of Death hovered above me, opening his greatcoat,
eager to scoop me up, lay me gently as any lover.
It was that close. I could smell him.

Bottle

The bottle of Parisian air sold for $80,000.
In Beijing he displayed it on a shelf as art, sticker still
attached like the lingering red after a slap to the cheek, held it
high on a street as a silent protest to the city's grey air, thick with
>particulates.

What if he uncorked the bottle?
Would the air hiss and slither, curling upward
like leisurely smoke from the night's last cigarette?
Or disperse like a man who gives the slip to the detective tracking
>him?

How do objects store memories?
A trick to ensure the next generation keeps the chipped teapot,
the figurine with the missing foot?
Is there a compartment like the tiny box on a poison ring,

that reassures by its very existence?
I am envious of absolute faith, the certainty that dropping coins
>into a charity box
results in the elevation of the soul.
When my father died, his pacemaker kept trilling for a minute.

Was it to allow the soul to untether from the body?
I raised my eyes to the hospital ceiling to see if I could catch it
>drifting,
then lowered my ear to his chest to check for beats.

My friend collects perfume bottles: an apple, a castle, a woman's
curved torso.

If she opens the right one she'll be wrapped in midnight chiffon,
a New Year's Eve party, circa 1900.

Playing *Skachi* in Siberia

When I pictured Siberia, it was a vast landscape
of snow with birch and pine forests.
Other Americans conjure only black and white
gulags strewn across a never-changing backdrop.

Now in a taxi bumping along in deep winter.
Although we are not far from Ulan-Ude and I sit
between colleagues, I start to wonder if we will
ever arrive and how my husband (sixteen hours behind)
would be notified should the taxi veer off this narrow road
and slam into a tree.

We stop on a dark street. When the gate refuses
to open, a phone call brings forth the homeowner.
Soon three Buryat women, an older man, and I
sprawl on the floor to play a game.

Rules are explained, each player assigned a token
based on shape and color: one gnarled, another
a dark shade (difficult to differentiate).
The host throws: two lines stretch across the floorboards.
At first I do not recognize the pieces as horse vertebrae.
Then I hear the clattering of hooves and freeze
waiting for men to burst in, sabers swinging.

Stumbling onto the Stolpersteine Project, Berlin

> *A person is only forgotten*
> *when his or her name is forgotten.*
> —from The Talmud

No Mercedes in the garage.
No Braun coffee grinder to wake up the day.
We were a no German household.

Fifty years after my childhood,
I walk through Berlin on a gray, drizzled day.
A block of bland apartment buildings.
Turkish grocery on the corner with a man in a *kufi*
guarding piles of tired mandarins and battered apples.
What makes me stop?
I look down. Two small brass squares:
Vera. Rudolf.
Born. Deported. Murdered.

All around espresso machines whir
from inside cafes. Two teenagers laugh,
arms linked as they swing down the street.
Over 43,000 stones laid.
They call it *stumbling against forgetting*.
But in the rush forward,

how many stop to look?
Pedestrians hustle past.

Startled by the sound of German,
I look up for a moment,
then continue on, eyes down.

First Wife

Fifteen years into this marriage,
my teenagers click to find her photo,
call to me behind their closed door.
I lean in, turn away in embarrassment,
as if she could see me.
She took his name; I never did.
Thirty years on, she uses it still, Jewish a step
up from Italian, our husband claims.
My children with his surname too.

She never remarried, had none of her own.
As this marriage frays, I wonder about the first.
On a stool, I reach far into a kitchen cabinet
for what survived: a shamelessly blue teapot,
curved spout, its round cheeks smooth, handle
strangled with wrapped bamboo.

Nothing Left to Do

The children overtake us,
whether at twelve or twenty,

shedding shirts too short in the sleeves
or pants with hems fringed like *tzitzit*.

Their shadows scatter to continue games
played long after dark, the boys tumbling

in a mock fight; the little sister left out,
though years of anger are slow to fade.

I want to give them heirlooms now,
the two sets of silverware—

wedding presents to the great grandparents,
the injunction against mixing milk and meat.

Why wait until I'm gone?

The siblings gather over the holidays,
peer closely at the childhood photos as if

to see into the future, to believe what
they'll become.

Happyville

Maybe this plan was doomed from the start.
Even without God, we Jews believe in
tikkun olam, repairing the world.
In 1905 a group purchased a 2,200-
acre plantation in Aiken County, South Carolina,
dreaming of a utopian society.
What do Jews know of farming?
They tried their best: wrangled
sandy soil into pastures; harvested timber,
built a grist mill, a sawmill, a cotton gin.
Must everything be a lesson? A curse?
These Russian and Polish immigrants
knew not from farming.
Idealism sustained them, until.
Heavy rains washed out the fields.
Mud seeped into the houses, windows leaked.
The dam built to power the ginnery collapsed.
Each a disaster of biblical proportions,
though these socialists did not hold to such stories.
Debt sucked them down; new members did not flock in.
Three years later, they auctioned off
the livestock and equipment,
sold the farmland and left.
Now, 115 years later, another farmer
turns the soil, plows these fields edged by forest and lake.
All that remains of this experiment in happiness
a rusted tractor and the bones of a house.

Master Class

Each participant has paid good money for this:
the retired Korean engineer training for
a second career as a church soloist, an Armenian
immigrant who attempts a Donizetti aria, the young
ingénue wavering between pop and an uncertain classical career.

The opera coach stands before us,
curves his fingers upward into a cathedral arch
to demonstrate how the first singer must widen her mouth.
He takes her torso, turns it to position the body as if for attack,
the voice an arrow aimed at a far-off target.
The audience motionless, attentive, though in truth
we are more like fans cheering the home team.

Introduced to the coach, I am nervous as if on audition.
I blurt out how my brother was a boy soprano
in the San Francisco Opera, as if this gives me legitimacy,
worried that any minute this man will discover
I can't keep pitch, exposing me in front of everyone.

My palms are beginning to sweat, the pleasure of Puccini's
"O mio babbino caro" lost to the anxiety of whether
the singers will hit their high notes.
They may not be here for applause, but isn't that what we all want,
if only once: to be tossed a bouquet onstage, cheered and greeted
by throngs of well-wishers at the stage door.

Notes

Several poems in part IV are based on paintings by Lucian Freud "Big Sue," "*Interior at Paddington,*" "*Animal under the Clothes,*" "*Benefits Supervisor Sleeping,*" "*Evening in the Studio,*" "*Girl with a Kitten,*" "*Painter's Mother Resting III,*" "*Queen Elizabeth II,*" and "*Painter's Mother IV.*"

The Stolpersteine Project (from German, meaning "stumbling stone") was initiated by the German artist Gunter Demnig in 1992 and is still ongoing. It aims to remember victims of Nazi terror by installing brass plaques in the pavement in front of victims' last residency of choice. As of January 2015, over 50,000 stolpersteine have been laid in 610 places in Germany and in 18 European and Scandinavian countries. As Deming said, it is "An art project that commemorates the victims of National Socialism, keeping alive the memory of all Jews, Roma and Sinti, homosexuals, dissidents, Jehovah's Witnesses and victims of euthanasia who were deported and exterminated." This also includes minorities, members of the Christian opposition (both Protestants and Catholics), the Communist Party and the European anti-Nazi Resistance, military deserters and the physically or mentally disabled.

Each piece is a cobblestone-size concrete cube bearing a brass plate inscribed with the name and dates of the victims of Nazi extermination. Demnig cites the Talmud, saying that "A person is only forgotten when his or her name is forgotten." The Stolpersteine in front of the buildings bring back to memory the people who once lived there. Each stone says: *Here lived ... Deported, Murdered*

Glossary

Hamsa: An ancient Middle Eastern amulet symbolizing the Hand of God. In all faiths it is a protective sign. It brings its owner happiness, luck, health, and good fortune..

Kinehora: A contraction of three Yiddish words: *kayn ayin hara*, a Yiddish expression used to ward off a jinx or to fool the evil eye. When people talk about their gains, they say *kinehora* so the evil eye will not act.

Kufi: A cap worn by men in North Africa and the Middle East. Also called *taqiyah*.

Shiva: The first seven days of mourning that follows burial. Usually the mourners do not leave the house.

Shmita: The seventh year of an agricultural cycle when the land is left fallow and planting, plowing, etc. are forbidden by *halakha* (Jewish law).

Tzitzit: Fringed tassels on the corners of a prayer shawl (*tallit*) or undergarment.

About the Author

Carol V. Davis is the author of *Between Storms* (Truman State University Press, 2012) and won the 2007 T. S. Eliot Prize for *Into the Arms of Pushkin: Poems of St. Petersburg* (TSUP). *It's Time to Talk About* was published in a bilingual English/Russian edition (Symposium, Russia (1997).

Twice a Fulbright scholar in Russia, Davis has taught in Michigan and Russia, and now teaches at Santa Monica College and Antioch University, Los Angeles. In winter 2015, she taught in Ulan-Ude, Buryatia Republic, Siberia. Her poetry has been read on NPR, Radio Russia, and she has read at the Library of Congress.